Home and school working together

Research shows that the greatest influence on children's education co[illegible] how much schools do to raise achievement, the thing that really make[illegible] parents who are **interested**.

Most parents are very interested: the problem is that they don't all kno[illegible] what the government **expects** in Literacy of Year 1 children — or how they can best help their child achieve those expectations. This book will:

- Explain some of the new teaching methods and tell you what is expected of your child in Literacy in Year 1.
- Show what support you can give at home which will really make a difference to your child's education.

If at any time you are worried about your child's progress, it is important to talk with the teacher sooner rather than later.

Is Year 1 the same in every school?

Schools deliver the curriculum in different ways: the activities suggested in this book will support your child's learning no matter what schemes or programmes the school follows. They will:

- Develop the **skills** that your child needs to learn Literacy.
- Develop the **concentration** which is so essential for learning.

The activities are designed to be fun and a bit different from the usual activities at school — so that your child will still be fresh and excited when he/she meets school-work the next day.

Play is the way to learn

It is through play that your child develops the skills he/she needs for more formal learning in school. All kinds of play develop Literacy skills — indoor and outdoor games, imaginative play with toys, dressing up, acting out stories, playing with friends and playing alone. Each section of this book will show you which skills your child is developing with each type of play.

Make the most of learning opportunities in everyday life

We are all so busy these days that many parents cannot find the time to sit down and do as much as they would like to with their children.

Jigsaw will show you how to use the many opportunities there are to develop your child's Literacy skills while going about your normal daily life.

Do we expect too much of Year 1 children?

Children develop at different rates. Your child will, at times, make rapid academic progress, and at others times appear to stay still academically, while developing in other ways — perhaps emotionally or physically. It is important to have realistic expectations of him/her and not to panic because another child in the class is reading Harry Potter!

Throughout this book the **national expectations of children by the end of Year 1 in Literacy** are printed in blue so that you can see clearly what teachers are teaching. Throughout the year they will be assessing your child against these expectations.

You will see that for many of the expectations — particularly in Speaking and Listening — it is **you** who will really make the difference to your child's achievement. After all, the teacher has to listen to thirty children! However big your family — it can't be that demanding!

Children are like seeds

If you are a gardener you probably know that you can try to get an early harvest by sowing some seeds in January. You have to keep them covered and warm, bring them in at night and put them out again in the morning, until May. It is hard work and many of the seedlings wither along the way.

If you wait until April and sow the same seeds outside **when conditions are right** you need do very little. Most seeds will germinate and grow happily without much attention. And you get your harvest at much the same time as those seeds that gave you all the hard work.

It is similar with children. Plant them in formal education before they are ready and you will have to work very hard to teach them. Some will survive. But many children who have not reached the developmental stages (visual and auditory discrimination, fine motor control etc.) to be **ready to learn** will fall by the wayside. Boys in particular often take longer to acquire language skills and can become disheartened by 'failing' in comparison with girls. In the worst cases, such boys give up trying and become disruptive.

If you wait until children are **ready** for formal learning almost all will flourish — and be reading and writing confidently at roughly the same time as those who started early.

Remember that in some European countries children do not even start formal school until the age of seven — and then they learn to read and write very quickly. In this country we start children much earlier and then work very hard to teach them.

But we should not just **wait** until children are ready. We should provide them with all the activities they need to develop the skills for reading and writing. Then they will be **ready** to learn to read and write quickly, rather than with a lot of anxiety and heartache from starting too early.

Speaking and Listening

The teachers' guide, The Primary Framework for Literacy, tells them to devote **one third** of class Literacy time to Speaking and Listening — it is every bit as important as Reading and Writing because, of course, it is through speaking and listening that children learn every other subject at school.

Most of us probably think our children talk too much and don't listen enough — so we'll deal with listening first. (Teachers often feel the same!)

Listening

It is easy to see that nowadays it is more difficult for children to learn how to listen properly for all sorts of reasons, including these:

- Most homes have background noise from radios and TV. This makes it hard for children to work out what needs to be listened to and what they can ignore (or perhaps we should say what they **want** to listen to and what they **choose** to ignore!)
- Most families are much busier than they used to be and it takes **time** to talk with children — both to explain things properly to them and to listen while they try to explain themselves.
- The traditional times that families talk to each other, such as mealtimes, do not always happen nowadays.

Children used to learn to speak and listen at home and then go to school to learn to read and write — but now the schools have to teach many of them to speak and listen as well!

Does your child always look at you when you speak?

Very many children don't! Teachers find that they have to teach children how to listen, so it is useful if parents teach children to:

- stop what they are doing,
- look at the person speaking, and
- keep listening until the speaker finishes.

There are some children in every class who are sitting quietly but not really listening properly — so they are not learning as much as they could. Try to make sure that your child isn't one of them — by teaching him/her to listen well.

English as an Additional Language (E.A.L.)

E.A.L. children must continue to develop speaking and listening skills in their **first** language at home as well. Speaking their first language to a high standard enables them to do the **thinking** required in other subjects, such as Maths and Science. It also helps their development as English speakers, readers and writers.

Listening and Responding

By the end of Year 1 children are expected to:

- **Listen to and follow instructions accurately, asking for help and clarification if necessary.**

One example of this would be if you said to your child, "Tidy up now — put your toys in the box, the books on the shelf and the crayons in the pencil case. Then come and help lay the table."

Your child might then ask, "Which side does the knife go?"

Practise by giving your child one or two instructions at a time to start with, and then a list of three or four things to do as he/she becomes better at listening and doing what you say.

So — when you are getting exasperated with your child not following instructions, try to calm down, speak clearly and watch to make sure your child does it, rather than rush on to the next thing! Not only will you be training your child, but helping him/her to achieve the Literacy expectations for Year 1.

- **Listen with sustained concentration, building new stores of words in different contexts.**
- **Experiment with and build new stores of words to communicate in different contexts**

These mean:

1. Talking with your child while you're doing all sorts of things — going round the supermarket, doing the housework, on outings and so on. Expect him/her to listen and then reply to you — in short, just have conversations! Your child will gradually learn all sorts of new words and will become better at reading comprehension and writing, as well as speaking and listening.

2. Listening to stories and talking about them. This is essential for your child's development — in Literacy and in many other ways.

We'll look at this properly in the section on Reading.

- **Listen to tapes or video and express views about how a story or information has been presented.**

The reason why sitting in front of a TV for hours on end (as so many children do) is not good for them is that the TV isn't **interested** in them. If a child watches with a parent who then talks about the programme it is different — TV can be a wonderful way of finding out about the world and learning new vocabulary. So choose interesting programmes, explain new words and talk about what you have watched — you will be helping to achieve the Year 1 expectations!

Group discussion

Children are expected to express themselves in all sorts of school activities, such as drama, discussion, and explaining their work in Maths, Science, and other subjects.

You will see how easy the expectations are to satisfy at home. Really it is just the kind of normal family talk that should go on in all homes.

By the end of Year 1 children should be able to:

- **Take turns to speak, listen to others' suggestions and talk about what they are going to do.**

For example, you might give your children and friends a plastic tablecloth, some old plates and cups and some play-dough (or real food) to make a Teddy Bears' Picnic. With any luck they will just get on with it — fetching their teddies, planning what food to make and collecting water for the drinks. If they are not actually taking turns and listening to each other, you will need to encourage them to do so.

- **Ask and answer questions, make relevant contributions, offer suggestions and take turns.**

The children might ask you (or each other) how to make a cheese and salad sandwich (with real food or play-dough). Others might be able to explain how, or suggest something else. They need to take turns to speak and listen to each other.

- **Explain their views to others in a small group; decide how to report the group's views to the class.**

Children will probably explain to each other their ideas about how to organise the picnic. Then they can come back and tell you what they have decided and what else they need.

Play is the way

Holding a Teddy Bears' Picnic is one example of play that develops the speaking, listening and social skills that are expected of your child in Year 1.

You and your child will be able to think of other play situations to achieve the same result — a child who confidently explains him/herself, listens to others and takes turns.

Speaking

By the end of Year 1 children should be able to:

- **Tell stories and describe incidents from their own experience in an audible voice.**

This simply means finding the time to listen when your child tells you what has happened. The important point is that children need to speak loudly enough to be heard — a great many Year 1 children talk in whispers. The more you listen to your child, the more confident he/she will become — and you can gently encourage louder speaking by pretending that you can't hear!

- **Interpret a text by reading aloud with some variety in pace and emphasis.**

Children need to use expression when they read aloud to make it interesting and not just flat and boring. The first stage of this is putting on voices for different characters.

- **Re-tell stories, ordering events using story language.**

The rest of the speaking expectations for Year 1 are linked with reading and we will look more closely at them later on. Children should be able to re-tell all those traditional stories, such as *The Three Little Pigs*, *The Billy Goats Gruff* and *Little Red Riding Hood*. There is a copy of *Goldilocks and The Three Bears* on the website, with pictures to cut out for your child to use when re-telling the story.

English as an Additional Language

Remember that E.A.L. children can do all the activities in their first language, for the reasons explained on Page **3**.

Drama

- **Explore familiar themes and characters through improvisation and role-play.**
- **Act out their own and well-known stories, using voices for characters.**

Throughout history children have loved dressing-up and putting on plays for their families — but TV and computers are now taking their toll on this valuable form of play. There is never time in school to do enough of it.

Collect old clothes, hats, and bags and let your child act out stories with brothers and sisters or friends. All that speaking and performing will do the world of good for your child's Literacy development. When they have practised their play, put chairs in a row and be an audience for them! You could suggest they make tickets too, or even draw pictures and write a cast list for a programme.

- **Discuss why they like a performance.**

Children simply say what they liked about each other's plays. Or your children could watch each other tell a story with pictures or puppets. (It is a good idea to show them how to comment on a performance first, by doing it yourself.)

Telling stories using small toys is another good way of putting on a performance — your child could set out the scene and then move around the characters as he/she tells the tale. Of course, you could always talk about a TV show you've watched together — that's another performance.

Reading

To be a good reader your child needs to do two things:

- work out what the words **say** – **c - a - t** sounds-out as **cat** (teachers call this "decoding" or "sounding-out")
- understand what the words **mean** (teachers call this "comprehension")

Many Year 1 children would be able to read aloud this sentence:

'A cat is a mammal.'

They may be able to sound-out the word 'mammal'. But, if they don't know that a mammal is 'an animal with hair which suckles its young' (and what that means) then they have not really understood it and have not **made sense** of the words.

So the two skills of reading for children to **make sense** of the words are

Decoding and **Comprehension**

(sounding-out the words) **(understanding what the words mean)**

When children are assessed on reading at the end of Year 2 they need both these reading skills.

Some parents worry a lot about how fast their children are learning to read in Year 1 and they are usually worrying about the decoding side of reading – the '**c-a-t** = **cat**' bit – because they see other children in the class on a more difficult book. But remember...

Rule Number One for Year 1 Parents:

DON'T WASTE TIME WORRYING.

Different children "take off" in learning to read at different times and worrying about it does no good at all. Often the ground work for reading is done in Year 1 and children take off and make rapid progress in Year 2.

Learning to read is not a race.

If your child is not yet ready to make quick progress with the **decoding** side of reading there are two main things you can do to help:

- Provide activities to develop decoding skills. We will look at these later on.
- While your child is practising these skills for decoding, develop his/her comprehension by **reading to** him/her. We will look at how to do this next.

Sharing books with your child

Schools often ask parents to "share a book with your child". It might be useful to see "sharing a book" with a Year 1 child in two separate ways:

- When **you** are reading to your **child**, you are helping to develop his/her **comprehension** skills.
- When your **child** is reading to **you**, the child is **decoding** and you are there to help when he/she gets stuck.

Although it is **decoding** that causes parents the most anxiety we will look at **comprehension** first because it is easy to develop your child's comprehension skills. After all, you have been helping him/her to understand words by talking since birth. And all the bedtime stories you have read have helped him/her to understand language and learn new vocabulary.

Also, most importantly, developing comprehension skills should be completely stress-free for your child, as it simply involves listening to stories and talking with the person he/she loves most in the world.

It is interesting how children with good comprehension skills (and that usually means good speaking skills too) can do quite well in Year 2 assessments even if they still have difficulty working out a lot of words. They use all their knowledge of books and language, which their parents have helped them to build up from bedtime stories over the years. (If your child is not yet used to being read to, then start **now** — it's never too late!)

Reading to your child to develop understanding

Reading to your child and talking about the pictures and the story is the way to develop the comprehension skills he/she needs to do well at school and in assessments in Year 2. Every time you read to your child you are helping to develop his/her:

- vocabulary,
- imagination, and
- understanding of the world.

And you are also helping to improve your child's **writing**. Children who have had lots of stories **read** to them become better **writers**.

Try to read your to your child as often as you can during the day — sitting in waiting rooms, on the bus, and certainly a bedtime story every night.

Most importantly, **don't stop reading to your child when he/she begins to read confidently alone**. You need to keep reading aloud to continue developing your child's comprehension and vocabulary.

Using picture books to develop comprehension

There are hundreds of wonderful stories around and the more you read, the more you will enjoy them, even as an adult! They are ideal for satisfying the expectations that at the end of Year 1 a child should be able to:

- **Identify the main events and characters in stories.**
- **Select books for personal reading and give reasons for choices.**
- **Visualise and comment on events, characters and ideas, making imaginative links to own experiences.**

For example, you might read your child this lovely story about what happens when the three bears come home and find that Goldilocks has been in their house.

First you would talk about the front cover and then spend time looking at the picture right at the front, before the story even starts. See if your child recognises the characters and works out that these are the three bears at the **end** of the story of Goldliocks.

You might then ask your child why Mummy Bear is looking shocked — and then what Baby Bear is feeling and how we can tell (sad — because he is holding his broken chair).

Then you could ask what your child thinks might happen on the next page, and so **make predictions showing an understanding of ideas, events and characters**. It doesn't matter if your child does not guess what actually does happen, as long as it is a reasonably sensible idea. You can have a guess too. Read on and see who is right! Ask the same kind of questions all the way through and you will have helped your child to **understand and interpret the text**.

Talk about the story as you go along. You are helping your child to **visualise and comment on events, characters and ideas**.

The bears in this story get their own back on Goldilocks, but there is a twist at the end (another opportunity for prediction). After reading you can discuss how the characters behaved and then talk about children your child knows who are naughty, or a time the house got in a terrible mess — so you are **making imaginative links to own experiences**.

You can easily adapt these ideas for other stories. The same kind of questions suit most stories — "What do you think will happen?" "What do you think .... feels?" "Was that a good thing to do or a silly thing?" "Which bit did you like best?" You'll be able to think of plenty more.

But, with all the pressure there is around nowadays in schools, do try to remember that the main reason for reading to your child is that it is a lovely thing to do, and don't make the bedtime story into a comprehension test! **Reading is for enjoyment, not work!**

Old favourites are still important!

The reason that traditional tales — such as *Goldilocks*, *Anansi the Spider* and *Little Red Riding Hood* — have been told all over the world for centuries is that they are so easy to remember and hand down to the next generation.

Language that is easy to remember is exactly what children need to become literate. Both the story-lines and the sentences of folk-tales and fairy-tales have so much repetition that the child soon wants to join in — long before he/she is able to read alone. These old stories are perfect for enabling children to satisfy the end of Year 1 expectation:

- **Re-tell stories, ordering events using story language.**

Examples of 'story language' include, "Once upon a time," and "The big, bad wolf".

Of course, children need to hear stories over and over again to be able to re-tell them. So when you lose the will to live because your child has asked for the same story so many times, just grit your teeth and try to enjoy putting on different voices!

English as an Additional Language

As explained on page **3**, children with English as an Additional Language should also retell these traditional tales in their first language as it will help develop their cognitive (thinking) skills.

Play is the way

Help your child to stick pictures onto card (cereal packs are fine). Then colour them, cut them out and fix them onto lolly sticks to make stick puppets.

You can make a puppet theatre by cutting one side out of a cardboard box.

When your child has practised, sit down and be the audience. Or even video it and produce a 'TV show'.

There is a copy of The Three Bears for you to download and make into a little book for your child on **www.jigsawbooks.co.uk**. There are also pictures to make into stick puppets.

Nursery rhymes and songs

Nursery rhymes are not just for nursery children. They are fantastic for helping children learn Literacy and have value all the way through Key Stage 1 and into Key Stage 2.

Children love rhythms and rhymes and enjoy finishing off lines as you read aloud, giving them a satisfying feeling of success, and developing confidence that they will soon be able to read independently.

Children who have a lot of experience of songs and nursery rhymes find learning to read easier — they recognise patterns in words and sounds.

Learning unusual words

Nursery rhymes are also important for learning new vocabulary. You will need to explain 'cobbler' and 'half a crown' if you teach your child this rhyme.

Cobbler, cobbler, mend my shoe,
Get it done by half past two.
Stitch it up and stitch it down,
And I will give you half a crown.

Later on in school, when your child meets those two words in novels, or in History topics, he/she will remember that a cobbler mends shoes and that half a crown was a coin — because of the rhyme. It fixes the word in a child's memory — much more permanently than if you had just explained what a cobbler was without teaching the nursery rhyme.

In Key Stage 2 Literacy lessons children are expected to recognise archaic language. Your child will be well ahead if he/she has a whole store of nursery rhymes to draw on.

Of course, there are references to nursery rhymes in a lot of classic books which children will meet later on. For example, they need to know *Mary, Mary, Quite Contrary* to understand parts of *The Secret Garden*. Nursery rhymes are part of the British cultural heritage and all children should learn them.

Developing memory

Learning by heart also develops memory and concentration skills, so use those times sitting in traffic jams or walking along the road to teach your child new nursery rhymes, poems and songs.

Both traditional tales and nursery rhymes will help your child meet the expectation:

- **Explain the effect of patterns of language and repeated words and phrases.**

This seems something of an over-expectation for Year 1: perhaps substitute the word 'enjoy' for 'explain'.

Read different types of book

You need to provide a wide range of books because your child is expected, by the end of Year 1, to:

- **Select books for personal reading and give reasons for choice.**

Unless you have an enormous selection of books at home, you'll need to join the local library. They are wonderful places: children love going to get their new books and stories on CD for the week.

Children can join libraries and take out books free so there is no reason to put off joining.

Information books

To **select books and give reasons** children need to have read plenty of information books (non-fiction) as well as stories.

Get your child used to finding factual books about everything he/she is interested in, from **A**rt, **B**ears and **C**ircuses to **X**-rays, **Y**achts and **Z**oos.

Children love factual books just as much as stories, and of course, by reading them you are developing your child's knowledge of the world, vocabulary and comprehension skills. By the end of Year 1 he/she should be able to:

- **Find specific information in simple texts.**

This just means that you show him/her how to use the contents page and the index to look up what you want to know.

Books with instructions

Look also for different kinds of non-fiction books — cookery books and other books with instructions, like art and craft books. The Year 1 expectation is:

- **Recognise the main elements that shape different texts.**

This means that children need to be familiar with all the different types of layout that non-fiction books have. They need to know how things like headings, sub-headings and lists help us to find our way around the book.

If your child has plenty of experience of using recipes to cook and instructions to make things, he/she will find questions on the layout of texts easy in Year 2 assessments.

You'll find instruction texts on the internet too. **www.bbc.co.uk/bluepeter** has plenty of ideas in its 'Things to do' section.

Poetry books

In the section on nursery rhymes we looked at why rhyme and rhythm are so important. In Year 1 your child will read poems which deal with the senses — seeing, hearing, feeling, tasting and touching — and also other poems on themes the teacher chooses.

Don't forget stories told in rhyme. The rhythm and rhyme make you want to keep on reading and it is easy to see why children love them.

Learning to tell fact from fiction

Your child will gradually work out what is real and what is not through reading books with you. By the end of Year 1 he/she should be able to:

- **Distinguish fiction and non-fiction texts and the different purposes for reading them.**

There are little bears.

- Sun Bears are the smallest bears.
- They weigh between 27 and 65 kg (60 to 145 lbs), and are 1.2 to 1.5 metres high/long (4 to 5 feet).
- Sun Bears are very rare.
- They live in the forests of South East Asia, where they are often kept as pets.

There are big bears.

- American Brown Bears, also called Grizzly Bears, are very big.
- They can weigh as much as 390 kg (800 lbs).
- However, the largest bear of all is the Polar Bear. It can weigh up to 600 kg (1,320 lbs) and is 2.4 to 2.6 metres (8 to 9 feet) tall/long.

Bears can be black.

- The Asiatic Black Bear lives in the forests and mountains of Asia.
- These bears have a golden crest on their chest and a mane of long black hair.
- There is also an American Black Bear, a large black bear with a brown muzzle.

Bears can be brown.

- The Brown Bear is the most common bear.
- Brown Bears live in Northern Canada and all over Russia.
- They have a distinct hump on their shoulders and very long claws on their front paws.

Bears, Bears, and More Bears

This is a beautifully illustrated information book, ideal for Year 1 children. It has a simple text for your child to read and more detailed information at the back, which you can read and explain.

How many bear books can you find?

You might like to start collecting bear books with your child and sort them into:

- fiction — stories about teddy bears and real bears who can talk like humans, and
- non-fiction — books for learning facts about real bears.

You can download book covers to make mini-books from **www.jigsawbooks.co.uk**. Your child could draw a picture of each bear and write the title and a bit about the book.

When your child starts reading

We have looked at how you can develop one reading skill, **comprehension**, by reading aloud to your child. The other skill of reading, **decoding**, means your child learning to blend each sound together, for example:

c – a – t sounds out as **cat**.

Some children in Year 1 start to work out the words without difficulty. But many find it hard, and it is not surprising — just imagine being five years old again and trying to **see** the difference between pairs of letters, such as:

> **Remember:** you need to say letter **sounds**: cuh - ah - tuh,
> not their names **C** (see) - **A** (ay) - **T** (tee)

b and **d** **p** and **q** **n** and **u**

or trying to **hear** the difference between **b** as in **bear** and **p** as in **pair**.

Your child needs to have well-developed skills in:

- **seeing** the difference between similar letters
- **hearing** the difference between similar sounds

Seeing the difference between similar letters

You can help by providing enjoyable activities to develop these skills, such as **dot-to-dot**, **spot the difference** and **find the odd one out**. You can download examples of useful activities from **www.jigsawbooks.co.uk**. You will find countless more in puzzle books and fun pads from pound shops.

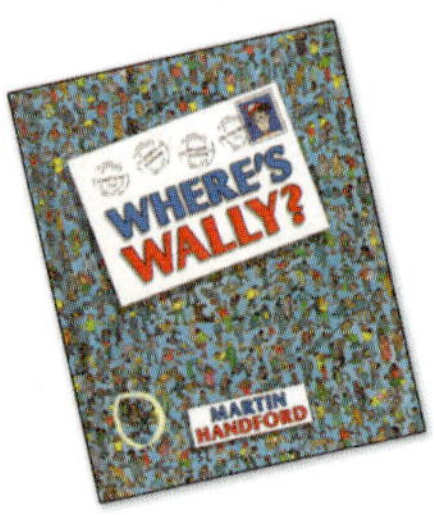

There are lots of books around where your child has to spot a small picture hidden in the main picture, or spot something on every page. Anything like this, which requires your child to look really carefully, will help prepare him/her for reading.

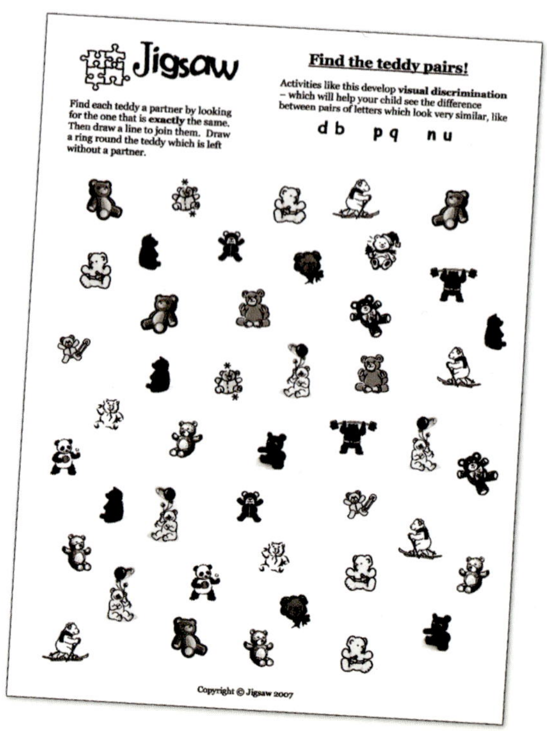

Jigsaw activities such as Find the Teddy Pairs are designed to lead your child closer to seeing the difference between reversed pairs of letters.

If he/she can see that  and  are facing opposite ways, it will sharpen eyesight and lead to seeing that so are **b** and **d**.

Spending too long on all those confusing letters before a child is **ready** to spot the difference can seem like a hopeless struggle. Using matching and spotting activities will sharpen your child's skills in an enjoyable way without turning him/her off reading.

Hearing the difference between similar sounds

Many children need a lot of practice at **listening** to be able to hear the difference between similar sounds — for example, to hear that the words

bear and **pear/pair** start with different sounds – **p** and **b**.

Listen to sounds around you

Listening is not the same as hearing — it is **making use** of your hearing. You can sharpen your child's skills by listening to environmental sounds. Get him/her to listen out for the difference between a helicopter and an aeroplane, the fridge and the washing machine, a bee and a fly — think of other similar pairs.

Listen out for rhymes

Listening carefully for rhymes is an early stage in learning to read. Your child needs to enjoy rhymes and predict them. All those nursery rhymes will have given him/her practice. But many children get confused about rhyme and think that it is the **first** sound in the word, so will hear the words

bear, **paw**, and **pair**

and think that **paw** and **pair** rhyme. But they need to listen to the sound at the **end**, because, of course, it is **bear** and **pair** that rhyme.

Make sure that your child is listening for the sound at the end of the word, and have fun making up rhymes and playing around with words. It doesn't even matter if the words make sense: it is the rhyme that matters for reading skills. Read the story of *Chicken Licken and Henny Penny*. Then invent names for favourite toys — 'Freddy Teddy', 'Rabbit Babbit', 'Funky Monkey' and so on!

Play is the way: Rhyming games

You can download rhyming games from **www.jigsawbooks.co.uk** or your child can make a game, by cutting out pictures from catalogues to make rhyming pairs. The spelling of the words doesn't matter — only that they rhyme. For example: paw and door, bear and chair, plane and train.

Invent games, such as:

- **Odd One Out** — hide one card first, spread the others out and ask your child to pick up all the pairs which rhyme. When there is only one left, the child guesses the hidden card from its rhyming pair.
- **Rhyming Bingo** — each child is given six cards which he/she lays out in front. Children turn over the pile of other cards one by one, and any child who has a picture that rhymes turns it over. The winner is the first to turn over all six cards.

Books that play around with language, such as *We're Going on a Bear Hunt*, enable children to experiment with different voices and speech sounds — "Swishy swashy," "Splash splosh," "Squelch squerch" — and are excellent for developing Literacy skills.

Tongue twisters

Enjoy tongue twisters like *Peter Piper picked a peck of pickled pepper* and *She sells sea shells by the sea shore*. Try inventing others with your child. He/she will start to recognise alliteration (where all words start with the same letter), which is important later on in Literacy.

How reading is taught now

You might have heard a lot on the news about 'synthetic phonics'. The government now recommends that 'high quality phonic work' should be the main method for teaching reading. But it also points out that, "**the more words children know and understand before they start on a systematic programme of phonic work, the better equipped they are to succeed.**"

So even if your child is learning to read through a phonics programme, he/she needs the wide vocabulary that comes from:

- talking with you in different situations about all sorts of things, and
- listening to bedtime stories.

Important words to understand

Two words which have been introduced recently are **phoneme** and **grapheme**. In some schools Year 1 children are taught to use these words, so you may need to understand them too!

A **phoneme** is a sound. A **grapheme** is the letter or group of letters which represent a sound.

In other schools children still call phonemes **sounds** and graphemes **letters** or **groups of letters**.

We have already looked at how to sharpen your child's listening to distinguish different sounds — which is so important in learning to read through phonics. He/she needs to be able to pick out each different sound in a word to hear that:

- cat has three different sounds — c - a - t — and three graphemes,
- bear has two different sounds — b - ear — and two graphemes (but four letters),
- teddy has four different sounds — t - e - dd - y — and four graphemes (but five letters), and
- picnic has six different sounds — p - i - c - n - i - c — and six graphemes.

There are **44** different sounds for children to learn quickly in Year 1 so that they can get on with reading.

Try reading these words aloud. They all have the same **phoneme**:

day rain late weigh

But each of the four words has a different **grapheme**:

ay ai a-e eigh

No wonder some children find reading difficult. That was an easy example; some phonemes can be written in **ten** different ways!

But that's not the only problem, because there are also different **phonemes** for the same **grapheme**: the grapheme **ear** sounds different in each of these words:

ear, bear, heart, and **heard.**

Splitting words into sounds for reading

Children are shown how to split words into separate sounds:

T - e - dd - y   b - ear - s'   p - i - c - n - i - c

Talk like a robot!

Teachers teach children to do 'sound talk'. Some call it 'toy talk' or 'robot talk'. Ask your child to show you how, and do more at home for extra practice. Sound talk is done by sounding out each phoneme and raising a finger as you say it. Then you say the whole word straight afterwards. The child gets the idea of splitting words up and then blending them back together — which is what they need to do when they read.

Your child might ask, **"What's for tea?"**

You could reply, **"E-gg-s eggs, b-ea-n-s beans, a-n-d and ch-i-p-s chips."**

Children enjoy talking like robots and you'll soon get the hang of it!

The expectations are that by the end of Year 1 children will:

- **Recognise and use alternative ways of pronouncing the graphemes already taught**
- **Recognise and use alternative ways of spelling the graphemes already taught**
- **Identify the constituent parts of two-syllable and three-syllable words to support the application of phonic knowledge and skills**
- **Recognise automatically an increasing number of familiar high frequency words**
- **Apply phonic knowledge and skills as the prime approach to reading and spelling unfamiliar words that are not completely decodable**
- **Read more challenging texts which can be decoded using their acquired phonic knowledge and skills, along with automatic recognition of high frequency words**
- **Read and spell phonically decodable two-syllable and three-syllable words**

Basically, all these expectations put together just mean that your child should:

- **work out the sounds** in order to read two-syllable words like c-o-tt-a-ge and three syllable words like ch-i-m-p-a-n-z-ee
- **recognise by sight** the most common 'tricky' words which don't sound-out easily, such as **said**, **there** and **come**.

Then he/she needs to use these two methods to read more challenging books.

Other ways to help with reading

Phonics has now hit the headlines as the recommended method for teaching reading, but it is not new. Sensible teachers have always used phonics alongside a range of other methods. It is important not to throw the baby out with the bathwater just because the phonics method is in fashion — other tried and tested ways still have their place.

Choosing books for your child to read

Of course, you should let your child have some choice when you visit the library, but we all know that children don't always know what's good for them! They often choose books that are too difficult, and sadly this can be because they become anxious when they see other children reading harder books. Look out for:

- Books with pictures to help tell the story.
- Books which repeat the same words.
- Books that are not too difficult — too much challenge is not a good thing. Children learn to read more quickly by reading lots of books which are reasonably easy for them — not by struggling through books which are too hard.

When you start a new book

- Read it to your child first, pointing to the words as you go along, and talk about the parts he/she enjoys.
- When your child reads, praise him/her as you go by making little comments like, "That was clever to work out that word," and "You *are* doing well!"
- Don't jump in to help as soon as your child stumbles over a word — children need time to work words out. But you need to keep the story flowing, so if the word really is too hard, then help. You could say, "What sound does it start/end with?" or "Try reading to the end of the sentence and then think again." The Year 1 expectation puts this, **"Use syntax and context when reading for meaning."**
- Let your child notice his/her own mistakes and put them right. We all learn from making mistakes and correcting them. If your child goes on reading and it doesn't make sense, point it out gently and show why that must be the wrong word.
- Suggest using the pictures as clues if he/she is really stuck on a word — it's not cheating!
- Remember that children are really strange — they can read a word one day and forget it the next. They can even read a word on one **page** and forget it the next. You just have to try very hard not to get annoyed — however tired you are!
- Never let your child get stressed about reading and never let him/her know if you are worried about progress. Find a good time to talk to the teacher about it.

When your child can read a new book

Suggest he/she reads it again to a brother or sister, or even to a teddy, to give more practice and fix the new words learnt in his/her memory. Reading it again will give your child confidence.

Little and often is the best way to learn and five to ten minutes reading is enough in Year 1, after a tiring day at school — but it needs to be every day. Of course, listening to stories isn't tiring, so **you** can read to your child for longer than that!

Spelling

Spelling is the reverse of reading

- To **read** the word **teddy** your child needs to say each sound he/she sees — **t-e-dd-y** — and then blend them together to make the whole word.
- To **spell** the word **teddy** he/she needs to say each sound in turn and remember which letters are needed to write it.

So spelling is more difficult, because the child needs to **remember** the letters. And spelling comes **after** reading as children obviously need to be able to read a word in order to remember the letters.

Don't ask your child to write the words straight away

It is best to do spelling games using magnetic letters (tape them at the back to make graphemes if you need more than one letter) or grapheme cards (which you can find at **www.jigsawbooks.co.uk**) rather than expecting your child to **write** the words — many Year 1 children will struggle if they have to think about how to write at the same time as thinking about spelling.

Say each separate sound

When your child is writing a word it is very important that he/she says each sound out loud to make the word. At first your child will probably ask you for spellings, so **you** will say each sound – but encourage him/her to repeat the sounds as he/she writes the letters, so that it becomes automatic.

Set a challenge

Give your child a set of magnetic letters or grapheme cards and see how many different words he/she can make. Use sounds that the teacher has already introduced — most schools have a set programme of about five a week.

Your child should have plenty of practice playing around and making words, changing one grapheme at a time and seeing how the word changes. For example, give this set:

sh, ch, th, ng, p, n, r, c, a, i

and your child can change one at a time to make:

ship, chip, chin, thin, than, can, cash, rash, rang, ring, rip, rich.

Or see how many words your child can make starting with **wh**, ending with **th** or that have, for example, **ew, ng,** or **ar** in them.

Gaining confidence in spelling

In most schools children are told to 'have a go' at spelling on their own before asking for help. It is a good idea to do this at home — otherwise your child may become dependent on you and feel that he/she cannot do it alone. Suggest first that he/she:

- sounds out the word and then, if still stuck,
- thinks of other similar words that may help — **some** is like **come**,
  could is like **would** and **should**.

There are lots of extra hints for spelling more tricky words; your child will learn other methods later. In Year 1 children are expected to:

- **Apply phonic knowledge and skills as the prime approach to reading and spelling unfamiliar words that are not completely decodable.**

Why don't teachers always correct spellings?

Parents often complain that teachers don't correct spellings, and Ofsted inspectors sometimes complain if a teacher corrects **too many** spellings: they think children will be put off writing if they feel too many words are wrong.

If your Year 1 child writes 'frend' for 'friend' then he/she is doing very well in phonics. Never cross it out. You might suggest that now he/she is such a good speller he/she can put the 'i' in next time to make it absolutely right.

National expectations for the end of Year 1 are:

- **Spell new words using phonics as the prime approach.**
- **Segment sounds into their constituent phonemes in order to spell them correctly.**
- **Recognise and use alternative ways of spelling the graphemes already taught.**
- **Spell phonically decodable two- and three-syllable words.**

All these just mean **split words up into sounds to spell them**. There is also:

- **Use knowledge of common inflections in spelling such as plurals, -ly, -er.**

Children would use phonics to work out those as well:

c-a-t-s   h-a-pp-i-l-y   t-ea-ch-er

The alphabet

Different schools teach the letter names — A (ay), B (bee), C (see), etc. — in different years. But children certainly need to know them for spelling. You can use magnetic letters at home, teaching the alphabet in chunks (you could stick a few together with masking tape) and then asking your child to put in the missing letters.

ABC??FGH   TU??XYZ

Handwriting

Your child needs fine motor skills (nimble fingers) to be able to form letters correctly. You can do a lot to help if your child is not quite ready do neat handwriting — by making sure he/she does plenty of 'fiddly' things to develop precision and hand–eye co-ordination.

Developing fine motor control without using a pencil

- Cutting out — show your child how to cut roughly round the edges to make the paper smaller before doing the intricate bit
- Sticking — managing small bits of paper and glue needs care!
- Sorting and making things with little beads
- Making models with plasticene and playdough
- Doing jigsaws with small pieces
- Sewing
- Playing with Lego, action figures, miniature cars and tiny toys
- Playing games with small pieces, such as Tiddlywinks
- Sorting coins, buttons and other small things into piles
- Tying shoe-laces and fastening buttons

Tear-a-bear: Tearing paper into small pieces is a challenge for Year 1 children, but makes lovely pictures. Show your child how to tear a little at a time and he/she will soon develop control over the paper. Start by making a bear's body, head and limbs separately and then sticking them together. Make a whole Teddy Bears' Picnic!

Activities using pencils, crayons, brushes or felt-tip pens

- Dot-to-dots
- Mazes
- Colouring-in
- Follow the lines
- Tracing
- Making and finishing patterns
- Painting
- Drawing

All these activities will develop pencil control and so improve your child's handwriting.

If children are not **ready** to write letters and words neatly, there is no point making them do more handwriting sheets. Let them have fun developing their fine motor skills in other ways — and then they'll succeed and enjoy the handwriting when they are ready.

The more children use their fingers, the sooner they will be ready to write neatly.

Holding the pencil the right way

It is essential that you show your child how to hold a pencil (or felt-tip or paintbrush) correctly right from the start. Bad habits are very hard to break and make handwriting more difficult. Don't assume the teacher will always have time to check.

Left-handed children should slant the paper the opposite way.

Forming letters

Different schools teach different handwriting schemes. It is important that you get a copy of the style used in your child's school or he/she may get confused. It is also worth making sure that you form the letters the same way as the teacher: schools may provide a sheet showing where the direction changes in each letter.

Cursive (joined) handwriting

Many schools teach joined handwriting, or the letters with the joining tags, in Year 1. There are many reasons this is thought to be a good thing. One reason is that that children do not have to worry about where each letter starts:

Printed

All the letters start in different places:

a b c d e f g h i j k l m
n o p q r s t u v w x y z

Cursive

When children first learn how to form the letters they all start on the line:

a b c d e f g h i j k l m
n o p q r s t u v w x y z

Learning to write letters involves a lot of watching

- First your child needs to **watch** how you form each letter. Then you might need to guide his/her hand to show all the changes of direction. After that he/she can trace on top of letters to practise and then copy them underneath.
- Then you need to **watch** your child to make sure that he/she forms them correctly.

Start forming letters in the air — not on paper

Before writing letters on paper your child needs to be sure of how to form each one. Ask for a sheet showing all the direction-changes for the style used in your school. Your child should form huge letters at first and gradually make them smaller.

- Try 'drawing' letters in the air with sticks or sparklers.
- Help your child to **feel** how each letter is formed by drawing it with a finger on the carpet, in sand, or in steam on the mirror at bath-time.
- Use chalks on paving, paints and felt tip pens to write big, colourful letters for fun, before using pencils to write smaller ones.

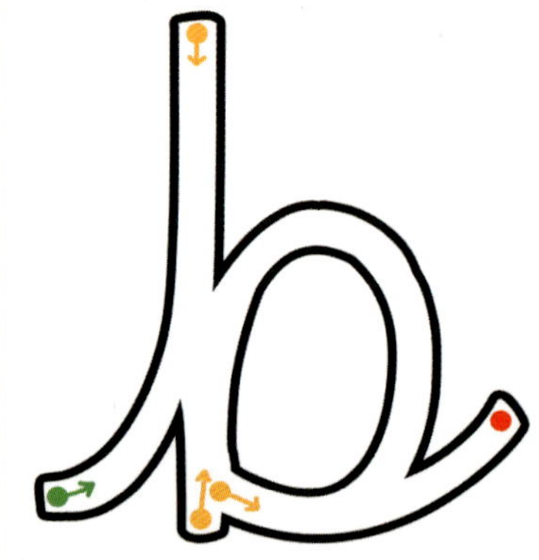

Does practice always make perfect?

Only if you are doing something the right way. If you practise doing something the **wrong** way you get perfect — at doing it wrong!

All those handwriting practice books that you can buy are only any use if you sit with your child the whole time, show how the letter is formed — and then **watch**. The book might keep your child quiet for a while, but it won't teach him/her how to form the letters.

Remember to make sure that the chair and table are at the right height so that your child has a straight back and feet resting on the floor. Use pencils, felt-tips or gel pens, but not biros as they are too thin and scratchy. Slant the paper so that your child can see the letters and the hand is not in the way.

The Year 1 expectations for Presentation (which includes handwriting) are:

- **Write most letters, correctly formed and orientated** (the right way around), **using a comfortable and efficient pencil grip.**
- **Write with spaces between words accurately.** Children can put a finger after each word to leave a space when first learning to write.
- **Use the space bar and keyboard to type name and simple text.** The earlier children start to find their way around a keyboard the better, so visit the library to use a computer if you don't have one at home.

Play is the way: Make a Teddy Bears' Picnic play-set

Shoe boxes can be covered with sticks or paper to make picnic baskets. Paper or plastic tablecloths can be decorated with felt-tips. Your child can make place cards or put names on paper plates — then decorate them. Then, of course there's cooking to do, or play-dough for the food.

Handwriting practice sheets can become boring, so, as soon as your child is forming the letters correctly, let him/her practise on more interesting things. He/she can write invitations to toys, make posters for the picnic and write thank you letters (from the toys) afterwards.

Keep everything together in the picnic basket and, with any luck, your child will play with it often, and for many peaceful hours!

Writing

Your child has been learning the skills for Literacy for years:

- **Listening** to you since birth
- **Speaking** from about one year old
- Developing **understanding** as a toddler by **being read to**
- Beginning to read by **decoding**
- Making words by **spelling**
- Learning to write the letters in **handwriting**

and all these skills come together in **writing** – the last and most difficult of the Literacy skills.

Did you know?

When teachers talk about writing they don't mean handwriting.

To be a good **writer** your child needs to have interesting thoughts, put them down on paper, and make sure they **make sense** to the reader by using punctuation.

Handwriting simply means forming the letters and words.

By the end of Year 1 children are expected to:

- **Independently choose what to write about, plan and follow it through**
- **Use key features of narrative in their own writing**
- **Convey information and ideas in simple non-narrative forms**
- **Find and use new and interesting words and phrases, including 'story language'**
- **Create short simple texts on paper and on screen which combine words with images (and sounds)**
- **Write chronological and non-chronological texts using simple structures**
- **Group written sentences together in chunks of meaning or subject**
- **Compose and write simple sentences independently to communicate meaning**
- **Use capital letters and full stops when punctuating simple sentences**

This all means that children should be able to:

- write different things, such as a very simple story with a title, or a caption to go with a picture,
- put capital letters and full-stops in the right places for sentences, and
- choose interesting words, for example, not, "**This is a toy,**" but, "**This is my best toy.**"

You can help at home by concentrating on making writing **enjoyable** for your child and showing all its different uses in daily life. Year 1 children really just need to do very short bits of writing at home – little and often, as with everything. For example, your child could write captions for photos in a scrapbook. If he/she is not ready to write, then let him/her do the thinking and tell **you** what to write – it is still good practice for writing.

Why is speaking so important for children's writing?

In order to write a sentence, your child needs to be able to say it first, in his/her head. Children who can tell you things – maybe about a story, a party or a game – find writing easier. Children who struggle to speak sentences usually find them hard to write as well. **Time spent talking with your child is well spent – for it also improves his/her writing.**

Play is the way

Invent games involving writing messages to each other. You could create a 'treasure hunt' by hiding a treat and leaving scraps of paper with clues: 'Look under the sofa,' 'On the window-sill,' etc. Then get your child to arrange a hunt for you, or for brothers and sisters.

Write letters from toys and put them in envelopes for your child to open. Your child can then write back and make stamps for the envelope. You could even make a postbox.

English as an Additional Language

It is important that children with E.A.L. have plenty of talk at home in their first language as well as speaking English, to develop their **thinking** skills. Having interesting conversations and discussing things in any language will lead to having lots of ideas for writing.

Let your child see what you write and how you write

When you write the shopping list, or the 'Gone out — dinner's in the oven' type of message, do the thinking **aloud**, so that your child sees that you need to compose the sentence in your head first. As you write, sound-out each part of the word to show how you make spelling easy. Give your child paper to write his/her own shopping list too.

Learning to write doesn't always need pencil and paper

As writing starts with composing sentences in the head, you can develop writing skills at any time — even when walking along the road. Try making up nonsense rhymes from nursery rhymes. This new version of an old rhyme is popular in schools now:

Baa baa, black sheep, have you any spots?
Yes Sir, yes Sir, I've got lots,
Some on my tummy, some on my toes,
And one very big one on the end of my nose.

Play with words

Invent silly rhymes using all your child's favourite nursery rhymes. Then he/she will find it easy when the class does poetry-writing. Try:

'Sing a song of ___________
A pocketful of ___________' or:

'Teddy bear, teddy bear,
Where have you been?'

You could write them down for your child and make a book.

Two very important points

- Always write in small (lower case) letters — *a b c d e* — not capitals — A B C D E — except to start sentences and names (of people, places, days, months and titles).
- Be careful if you use those workbooks that give children a sentence and tell them to put a full stop at the end. Putting a dot at the end of a line will not teach your child what a sentence is. He/she needs to learn to write sentences by reading lots of books.

A few basics (suggested by teachers)

Make sure your child gets enough sleep

This may seem obvious, but it is surprising how many children arrive at school each day too tired to learn properly. Some children who have televisions in their rooms watch unsuitable programmes long after they have been put to bed.

Many working parents try to do the right thing by their children but end up keeping them up too late. Better to read a really good story, get them to sleep, and do extra things in the morning, if they wake in time. Otherwise, leave activities until the weekend.

Get to school on time

Time-keeping is an important life-skill — and it starts with getting to school on time. Children who arrive in the playground a few minutes before the bell have time to say hello to friends, say goodbye to parents and go into school with everyone else. They are relaxed and ready to learn. Late-comers often start the day anxious and embarrassed, which is not good for learning.

Take the right equipment on the right day

Children who forget book-bags, P.E. kits and reply-slips feel uncomfortable about it. The teachers will nag them and often the whole class will be held up. Put everything ready for school next to your child's school shoes and then they should not be forgotten.